THE WORKING EXPERIENCE 3

BY JEANNE H. SMITH AND HARRY RINGEL

New Readers Press

ISBN 0-88336-967-2

Copyright © 1991
New Readers Press
Publishing Division of Laubach Literacy International
Box 131, Syracuse, New York 13210

Printed in the United States of America

Project Editor: Paula Schlusberg
Manuscript Editor: Maria Collis
Publication Assistant: Jeanna H. Walsh
Designer: Kathleen T. Bates
Cover design: The W. D. Burdick Company

9 8 7 6 5 4 3 2 1

Acknowledgments

The authors wish to express their sincere thanks to the following individuals and agencies without whose support *The Working Experience* would never have come to be:

Executive Directors Mike Blum and Rev. William Erat, of Nationalities Service Center and Lutheran Children and Family Service in Philadelphia, for providing the direction in their agencies which makes projects such as this one possible.

NSC Assistant Executive Director and Education Programs Coordinator Seki Howland, for her ongoing faith and input, especially as the role of LEA in this project evolved.

LCFS Community Services Manager Harriet Brener–Sam, for her support and interest in project direction.

Jim Biles and Barbara Buckley–Deni, instructors at Lutheran Children and Family Service, whose commitment and care were vital in preparing their students to be interviewed for this project.

JoAnn Weinberger, Executive Director of the Center for Literacy, Inc., who was always eager to listen to new ideas and willing to support our efforts.

Good Lad Inc. and Centro Pedro Claver, for extending the warmest of welcomes to our project.

The authors also extend their special thanks to all the ESL students who shared their working experiences and whose stories, which form the heart of *The Working Experience,* will now be shared with many others.

Table of Contents

How do you feel when you get paid?

Patty DiRienzo

Getting Paid

When I first got paid, I was very nervous. I didn't know how much I would get. I kept thinking, "What am I going to get?" But I was also happy because the money was mine. Before that, I had always depended on my husband. It felt so good to have money that was mine. I don't have to ask my mother for help anymore, either. Instead, when she needs help, I can give her something.

My country, Nicaragua, is very poor. I would like to work longer hours to make money and send it home to help my family there. But my husband won't let me work longer hours. He also says, "We need all the money we earn." But I don't care what he says. I would still like to send something to my sisters back home. Maybe someday I will.

In addition to getting paid, there are other things I like about my job. The benefits are good. The union is good. I want to become old working in this factory.

—**Yvonne Largaespada**
Nicaragua

Comprehension

True or False

Write **T** or **F** for true or false.

_____ 1. Yvonne was nervous when she first got paid.

_____ 2. Yvonne likes not having to depend on her husband.

_____ 3. Yvonne knew how much money she would get.

_____ 4. Yvonne has started to work longer hours.

_____ 5. Yvonne sends money to her sisters.

_____ 6. Yvonne wants to work someplace else.

Complete the Sentence

Fill in the blanks with the appropriate words and phrases from the story.

When I first got paid, I was very _____. I didn't know

_____ _____ I would get. But I was also

happy _____ the money was mine. Before that, I had always

_____ _____ my husband. Now, I don't

have to ask _____ _____ for help

anymore, _____. Instead, when she needs help, I can

_____ _____ _____.

Language Skills

Vocabulary Expansion

In the story Yvonne says, "The benefits are good." Benefits are extra payments that help workers for special reasons.

Below is a list of employee benefits that are sometimes given. (Remember: Not all employers offer all the possible benefits.)

vacation pay	health insurance
sick time	workman's compensation
overtime	disability
unemployment	bereavement
social security (required deduction)	

Read each of the statements below and fill in the blanks with the correct benefit.

1. Jack had to take three days of _____ because he had a fever and couldn't go to work.

2. Soon I will retire. I can collect my _____ benefits.

3. My grandmother died. I took two days _____ and stayed home to help with the funeral.

4. He got hurt on the job and can't work. He can collect _____.

5. Nilda will be paid two hours of _____ and eight hours of regular pay because she worked from eight AM until six PM.

6. Helen was laid off for two months. Her _____ check helped pay her bills.

7. John was in the hospital for a long time. He got paid _____ after he used his sick time.

8. Georgette cut her finger while cooking dinner. Her _____ paid for the stitches.

9. Maria got two weeks _____, and she went camping.

Punctuation: Quotation Marks

Quotation marks are placed around someone's exact words. When the exact words are not used, do not use quotation marks.

Example: Yvonne's husband says, "We need all the money we earn."

Some of the sentences below include someone's exact words. Others do not. Insert quotation marks where appropriate.

1. Yvonne says, I want to become old working in this factory.
2. Yvonne told us about her job.
3. Yvonne kept thinking, What am I going to get paid?
4. Yvonne tells us her sisters back home need help.

Follow-up

A Closer Look

Read each sentence. Study the underlined words. Answer the questions that follow.

1. Yvonne's husband says, "We need all the money we earn."

   How do people earn money?_____

   _____

2. Yvonne belongs to a union.

   What are some union activities? _____

   _____

3. Yvonne had always depended on her husband.

   Who do you depend on? _____

   _____

A Closer Look: Inference

The statements below refer to Yvonne's story, "Getting Paid." Decide whether each statement is true or false.

The information is not stated directly in the story. But you can find reasons in the story for your answers. You can agree or disagree with other students.

1. Yvonne is a young woman.
2. Her husband also works.
3. Yvonne used to get help from her mother.
4. Yvonne likes her job.
5. Yvonne's family is poor.
6. Yvonne generally does what her husband tells her to do.

Let's Talk about It

1. How did Yvonne feel when she got her first paycheck? Why?
2. Does Yvonne send money home to her family? Why or why not?
3. Why does Yvonne like her job?

What's Your Story?

How did you feel the first time you got a paycheck?

How does someone find a job in this country?

Patty DiRienzo

Job Hunting

Do you know how difficult it is for an immigrant to find a job in America? When I came here from China, I found that there were many differences in the ways to find a job.

When I went to work in China, it was no problem to find a job. I didn't need to write a resume and send it to many companies. After I finished college, the government arranged interviews with companies or factories that offered jobs to me. At first I wasn't able to find a position I wanted, but I didn't worry.

Now I have been in the United States for a year. During my job-hunting period, I have discovered that there are many differences. Here, I have to read the advertisements in the newspaper. First, I circle ads from companies which offer jobs I might want. Then I write many resumes and letters of application and send them to these companies.

Sometimes I am lucky, and I receive an appointment for an interview. When I can show the employer that I have the right qualifications, maybe I will get a job!

—Vincent Lei
China

Comprehension

True or False

Write **T** or **F** for true or false.

_____ 1. Many companies in China ask to see resumes from new workers.

_____ 2. In China, parents usually help their children to find a job.

_____ 3. In China, Vincent found a satisfying position immediately.

_____ 4. In America, Vincent uses a newspaper to help in his job hunting.

_____ 5. In America, qualifications are important for the jobs Vincent wants.

_____ 6. In America, Vincent always gets an interview when he applies for a job.

Multiple Choice

Circle the best way to complete each sentence.

1. Vincent is
    a. an American immigrant who wants to find a job in China.
    b. a Chinese immigrant looking for work in America.
    c. a college graduate who works for the Chinese government.

2. In China
    a. people don't go to college.
    b. the government finds jobs for some people.
    c. people must take the first job offer.

3. In America
    a. the government puts all job ads in the paper.
    b. companies do not want to see resumes.
    c. job qualifications are important.

4. During Vincent's job hunt in America, he
    a. wrote letters of application to every company that advertised.
    b. went for interviews before he sent resumes.
    c. read ads and sent resumes to companies where he wanted interviews.

Language Skills

Word Families

Write the verb forms for these nouns. The first three are in the story.

1. government   _____

2. appointment   _____

3. advertisement   _____

4. management`   _____

5. arrangement   _____

6. employment   _____

7. commitment   _____

Structure Practice: Time Signals

Write these time words from Vincent's story into the story below.

When   During   Now   First   Then   After

_____ I finished high school, I decided to go to college. I

have been at college for two years. _____ I first started

college, it was very difficult for me to write papers. _____

these two years, my writing has improved a lot. _____ I put

down all my thoughts. _____ I rewrite the whole piece to

improve the language. _____ I'm starting to enjoy writing

papers. If I continue to practice, maybe all my grades will improve!

Initials

Initials are the first letters in proper names of people, places, or things. Every person's name has initials. Write your initials here: _____

How many sets of initials do you recognize? Match initials below to their meanings.

1. FBI		a.	group of football teams
2. L.A.		b.	in the morning
3. USSR		c.	soldier in American army
4. NFL		d.	unidentified flying object
5. IRS		e.	large California city
6. AM		f.	"I Owe You" some money
7. GI		g.	national police department
8. IOU		h.	government agency that collects taxes
9. UFO		i.	Soviet Union

Vocabulary Review

Please write these words from Vincent's story into the story below.

resume	interview	job hunt
appointment	qualifications	ads

After I finished my job training program in auto mechanics, I began my

_____. To begin my search, I first looked at the Help Wanted

_____ in the newspaper. One car dealer had an opening, so I

called for information. The secretary asked for my _____ over

the phone. I told him I had been to training school but had no experience yet. He

told me I had to come in for an _____. I made an

_____ for Friday afternoon at 2:30. On Thursday night I typed

up my _____. But I didn't sleep that night. I was too worried!

Follow-up

A Closer Look

Read each sentence. Study the underlined words. Answer the questions that follow.

1. Vincent finds <u>ads</u> for jobs in the newspaper.

   What kind of information might you find in a job ad?

   _____

2. Vincent sends a <u>resume</u> and a letter of application when he wants to be considered for a job.

   What kinds of information should you put on a resume?

   _____

3. Sometimes, Vincent is invited in for a job <u>interview</u>.

   What are some things you can do to prepare for a job interview?

   _____

Let's Talk about It

1. Why was job hunting "no problem" for Vincent in China? Give at least two reasons.
2. Why is job hunting more difficult for Vincent in the U.S.? Give at least two reasons.
3. When Vincent couldn't find a job in China, why didn't he worry? Give your opinion.
4. What was the most important difference for Vincent between job hunting in China and in America? Give your opinion.

What's Your Story?

In your experience, how is job hunting in America different from job hunting in your country?

Robert Fox, Impact Visuals

Where I Work

The place where I work is a casino in Atlantic City. It is far from the city where I live. It takes me more than an hour to get there every day. But I enjoy commuting to Atlantic City. The drive is easy and relaxing. As I get close to work, the city is interesting to look at.

The casino is a tall, pink building. You can enjoy the lights shining from the building when you are on the expressway to Atlantic City, especially in the evening. At the end of the expressway, there is a huge parking lot for visitors and one for employees. A casino bus carries us to work from the expressway parking lot.

In front of the building there is an entrance for employees only. Every worker must show an ID card to get inside. Inside, the building has many different departments. For example, there are the business computer areas and the management offices. For customers there is also a swimming pool, a banquet room, a restaurant, and a night club. And, of course, there are the game rooms. A special heliport for helicopters is on top of the building.

The casino is an exciting, attractive place. It provides entertainment for a lot of people. But I only work there. I never gamble.

—**Tan Trinh**
Vietnam

Comprehension

True or False

Write **T** or **F** for true or false.

_____ 1. Tan lives near his job.

_____ 2. Tan doesn't mind commuting to work.

_____ 3. All employees park in a huge parking lot next to the casino.

_____ 4. The entrance for employees is on the side of the building.

_____ 5. After work every night, Tan usually gambles.

_____ 6. The employees use the casino swimming pool.

Complete the Sentence

Fill in the blanks with the appropriate words and phrases from the story.

The casino is a tall, pink _____. In front of the building

there is an _____ for employees only. Every worker must show

an _____ _____ to get inside. Inside, the

building has many different departments. There are the _____

_____ areas and the management offices. For customers

there is also a _____ _____, a banquet

room, a _____, and a night club. And, of course, there are the

_____ rooms.

Language Skills

Vocabulary Review

The following sentences use words from the story. Finish the sentences with your own words.

1. When I want entertainment, I usually _____.

2. _____ is an attractive place near where I live.

3. When people commute to work, they often _____.

4. When people gamble, they try to win _____.

5. People go to casinos in order to _____.

Structure Practice: Verbs

Write the **-ing** spellings for these verbs from the story. Remember to drop the final **e**.

1. live   _____

2. shine   _____

3. drive   _____

4. dance   _____

5. gamble   _____

Now use the **-ing** verbs you created to complete the sentences below. Note that the **-ing** form can sometimes be used as a noun or an adjective.

1. Tan likes _____ to Atlantic City.

2. The casino has rooms for _____ and _____.

3. At night, Vincent likes to look at the _____ lights of the city.

4. _____ far from work isn't always easy, but Tan manages.

Punctuation

Use commas when you write a list of people, places, or things.

Example: There is a swimming pool, a banquet room, a restaurant,
and a night club.

Now put commas into these sentences.

1. This class has people from Ethiopia Vietnam and Puerto Rico.

2. I always bring a notebook a pen and paper to class.

3. Students teachers and parents came to the meeting.

4. This house has one living room two bedrooms a kitchen and a bathroom.

5. My mother father sister and brother will live there.

Capitals: Cities

Sometimes names of cities are more than one word. Make sure to put capital letters
for both words.

Examples: Atlantic City   Buenos Aires

Rewrite the names of these cities with capital letters.

1. mexico city   _____

2. cape town   _____

3. hong kong   _____

4. los angeles   _____

5. san salvador   _____

Find two more city names with more than one word. You may use a map.

_____

_____

Follow-up

A Closer Look

Circle the one answer that does *not* go with the sentence.

1. Atlantic City has
   - a. shining lights.
   - b. large parking lots.
   - c. many mountains.
   - d. casinos.

2. Tan enjoys driving to Atlantic City because
   - a. the drive is easy and relaxing.
   - b. the city is interesting to look at.
   - c. the city is beautiful at night.
   - d. his girlfriend goes with him.

3. The departments in the casino where he works include
   - a. game rooms.
   - b. a small zoo.
   - c. computer areas.
   - d. management offices.

4. For entertainment, visitors to the casino can
   - a. play football on the roof.
   - b. use the swimming pool.
   - c. go dancing.
   - d. gamble in the game rooms.

Let's Talk about It

1. What kind of buildings are there in Atlantic City?
2. Why does Atlantic City need huge parking lots?
3. Why are the parking lots at the end of the expressway?
4. What can people do in the casino where Tan works?
5. Why do the employees have to show ID to enter the casino?
6. Why do many people come to Atlantic City?

What's Your Story?

What's a popular place in your town for entertainment? What kinds of jobs do people have there?

What would it be like to work at a car wash?

Cindy Reiman, Impact Visuals

Getting My First Job

I found my first job in America in 1982. At the time, my family was living in Los Angeles.

It happened like this.

I was riding on the bus with my friend Edward. It was going north on Vermont Avenue. Edward saw a Help Wanted sign in front of a place called Smith's Car Wash. We decided to stop and ask about the job.

At the time, there were just a few customers because it was Monday, the beginning of the week. We walked inside to the office of the owner of the car wash. Edward talked to him for me because I knew very little English.

All I remember about the owner of the car wash was that he asked me for my social security number and my age. I gave him the number and told him I was 27 years old. He also wanted to know about my experience. Well, I had to tell him that I had never washed a car before in my life.

After he heard all my answers, he told me, "The job is yours!"

The car wash was a good place to work. I stayed there for almost a year. Getting that job is something that I will never forget.

—**Juan Vegas**
Nicaragua

Comprehension

True or False

Write **T** or **F** for true or false.

_____ 1. Juan was alone when he saw a Help Wanted sign.

_____ 2. Juan got his first job as a car dealer.

_____ 3. Edward spoke English to the owner.

_____ 4. The owner asked Juan for his age.

_____ 5. Juan needed experience to get the job.

_____ 6. Juan worked in the car wash for five years.

Time Sequence

Number the events in Juan's story from **1** to **6** to show the order in which they happened. The first one is done for you.

_____ Juan and Edward went into the car wash to talk to the owner.

_____ The owner of the car wash gave Juan a job.

_____ Edward saw a Help Wanted sign in front of a car wash.

_____ Juan worked at the car wash for almost a year.

___1___ Juan and Edward were riding on a bus.

_____ The owner of the car wash asked Juan for his age and social security number.

Language Skills

Vocabulary Review

Place the correct word in the blank.

office   customers   social security number
sign   experience   owner

1. To get a job, you must often write your _____ on the application.

2. Companies usually put the name of their business on a large

   _____.

3. Stores always hope to have a lot of _____.

4. In a factory the supervisor usually has a private _____.

5. Someday Juan might be the _____ of his own car wash.

6. Having some _____ is usually helpful in getting a job.

Capitalization and Punctuation

Make letters capital where necessary and place periods where they belong in the following story selection:

i was riding on the bus with my friend edward it was going north on vermont avenue edward saw a help wanted sign in front of a place called smith's car wash we decided to stop and ask about the job

all i remember about the owner of the car wash was that he asked me for my social security number and my age i gave him the number and told him i was 27 years old

Structure Practice: Past and Past Continuous Tense

Circle the correct verb form.

1. Juan and his friend (rode, were riding) on a bus when they saw a car wash.

2. The owner (talked, was talking) on the telephone when we went into his office.

3. Edward (talked, was talking) to the owner in English.

4. I (was living, lived) in California when I got the job at the car wash.

5. Juan (worked, was working) at the car wash for almost a year.

Follow-up

Let's Talk about It

1. How did Juan learn about the job at the car wash?
2. Why did his friend Edward talk to the owner for Juan?
3. What did the owner want to know about Juan?
4. Why do you think the owner hired Juan?
5. Do you think Juan knew English better after almost one year at the car wash? Why or why not?

Thinking about the Story

What do you think are the reasons people are hired for a job?

What's Your Story?

Tell about how you got your first job in America. If you prefer, you can write about someone you know.

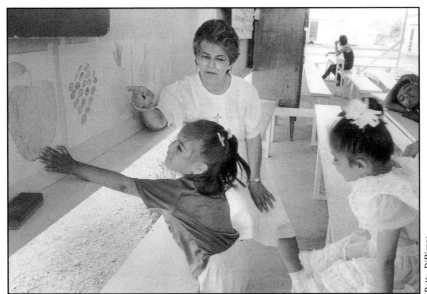

Patty DiRienzo

Nursery School Teacher

I have a B.A. degree in elementary education, and I also do social work. In Puerto Rico I worked as a teacher in a nursery school for children between three and five years old. The area where I worked is poor. The families in that area had no work or education.

The nursery school was funded by the government to help poor families.

We taught the children their letters and numbers. We played games with them so they could have exercise to develop their muscles. We also provided some counseling to the mothers and fathers to help them deal with family problems. The pay I earned from this job was low, but I liked the work.

—**Augustin Ortiz**
Puerto Rico

Comprehension

True or False

Write **T** or **F** for true or false.

_____ 1. Augustin has a college degree in elementary education.

_____ 2. He worked in a nursery school in a poor area.

_____ 3. The nursery school received private funding.

_____ 4. The children learned how to play musical instruments.

_____ 5. The parents received some counseling.

_____ 6. The job paid very well.

Multiple Choice

Circle the best way to complete each sentence.

1. Augustin worked in Puerto Rico as a
   a. doctor.
   b. factory worker.
   c. teacher.
   d. nurse.

2. The nursery school was funded by
   a. the government.
   b. the parents.
   c. the teachers.
   d. Augustin.

3. One thing Augustin did not do with the children was
   a. teach them letters.
   b. teach them numbers.
   c. play games.
   d. teach them religion.

4. The teachers also
   a. cooked lunch for the children.
   b. counseled the parents.
   c. drove the children home.
   d. taught music to the children.

Language Skills

Vocabulary

Circle the correct word in each sentence.

1. I have a B.A. in elementary education and I also do (social work, funding).

2. The (area, government) where I worked was poor.

3. We taught the (families, children) their letters and numbers.

4. We played games with them so they could have (experience, exercise) to develop their muscles.

5. We also provided some (counseling, classes) to the mothers and fathers to help them deal with family problems.

6. The pay I (worked, earned) from this job was bad, but I liked the work.

Structure Practice

Sometimes the word **to** introduces a verb phrase that gives a reason.

Examples: The nursery school was funded by the government to help poor families.

We provided counseling to the mothers and fathers to help them deal with family problems.

Complete the sentences below using your own words.

1. I came to this country to _____

_____.

2. I am studying English to _____

_____.

3. I want to earn money to _____

_____.

Vocabulary: Abbreviations

Abbreviations are often used for academic degrees. Match each abbreviation to its meaning.

Abbreviation	Meaning
B.A.	Bachelor of Arts—a four-year college degree
B.S.	General Equivalency Diploma or high school equivalency diploma
A.A.	Bachelor of Science—a four-year college degree
M.S.	Associate of Arts or Associates Degree—a two-year college degree usually from a community college
G.E.D.	Medical Doctor
M.D.	Master of Science
Ph.D.	A doctoral degree—follows the bachelor and master degrees

Follow-up

Let's Talk about It

1. How old were the children Augustin worked with?
2. What was the area like, and what was the condition of the families there?
3. Why did the nursery school teachers play games with the children?
4. How did they help the parents?
5. Why do you think Augustin liked the work?
6. What preparation did Augustin have for this job?

Thinking about the Story

Do you think it is better to have a job you like even if the pay isn't good, or to have a job you don't like where you earn a lot of money? Give reasons for your answer.

What's Your Story?

Are there programs in your country that help children and families? What are they like?

Out of Work

The pharmaceutical company that I worked for had some problems when inflation hit Mexico. Many companies closed down because they couldn't pay for products from overseas.

My company closed down. I had many problems getting another sales job like the one I'd had. Many of the companies didn't want to give me a similar job. When a person has worked in one company, it's very difficult for him to get a similar job with the same type of company. I don't know why this happens in Mexico, but this is the case with most companies.

There was another problem. In Mexico, when you are over 40 years old, many companies won't give you work. To those companies, you are an old man.

I mentioned my trouble to some friends in America. "It's different here," they wrote me. "Nobody tells 40-year-old people that they can't get a job." I liked that. It was a gamble, but I decided to move my family to America.

—Ruben Amaro
Mexico

Comprehension

True or False

Write **T** or **F** for true or false.

_____ 1. Ruben lost his job because his company fired him.

_____ 2. Ruben wanted to find a job as an engineer.

_____ 3. In Mexico, job experience with one company can hurt you if you try to find a similar job with another company.

_____ 4. In Ruben's opinion, it is easier for an older man to get a job in America than in Mexico.

Complete the Sentence

Fill in the blanks with the appropriate words and phrases from the story.

When inflation hit Mexico, many companies _____

_____ because they couldn't pay for _____

from overseas. My company closed down. I had many problems getting another

_____ _____. Many companies didn't

want to give me a _____ _____.

There was another _____. In Mexico, when you are over

_____ years old, many companies won't give you work. To

those companies, you are _____ _____

_____.

Language Skills

Structure Practice: Auxiliary Verbs

Auxiliary verbs, or helping verbs, are sometimes used to give special meanings to verbs. In some cases, they are used to change the tense or to make a verb negative.

Ruben uses some negative auxiliary verbs in his story.

Examples: couldn't pay   didn't want

                  can't get   won't give

Write these auxiliary verbs into the story below.

don't   didn't   couldn't   can't   won't   wouldn't

After Thomas lost his job, he _____ find work. He went to

many companies, but they _____ hire him. He was lost. He

_____ know what to do. So he called a friend in America. "I

_____ find any work here," Thomas complained. "What can I

do?" His friend told him to come to America. "You _____ have

the same problem here," his friend said. "And _____ worry!

I will help you."

Word Families

Write base verbs for these words from the story.

1. wrote   _____   5. happens   _____

2. losing   _____   6. worked   _____

3. tells   _____   7. had   _____

4. decided   _____   8. getting   _____

Vocabulary Review

Write these words into the story.

overseas   inflation   similar   gamble   mentions

When I get together with friends, someone always _____

the economy. We worry about money, because _____ causes

prices to go up all the time. We wonder if economic problems are

_____ in countries _____. Trying to make a

living in this country sometimes seems like one big _____.

Follow-up

A Closer Look

Circle the answer which you think best explains the meaning of the underlined word in each sentence. Look back at the story if you need help.

1. Many companies closed down because they couldn't pay.
   a. problems
   b. companies
   c. products
   d. inflation

2. I had trouble getting a sales job like the one I had.
   a. company
   b. trouble
   c. sales job
   d. product

3. I don't know why this happens in Mexico.
   a. companies close down
   b. some companies go into the same business
   c. companies buy products from overseas
   d. workers in one job have trouble finding a similar job

4. I liked that.
    a. friends in America
    b. 40-year-old people getting jobs in America
    c. old men being bosses of most companies in Mexico
    d. having different troubles in America

5. It was a gamble.
    a. moving to America to be with friends
    b. retiring at age 40
    c. moving to America to find a better job
    d. having a large family

Let's Talk about It

1. How did inflation create a problem for Ruben's company?
2. Why did Ruben have a problem finding work when his company closed down? Give two reasons.
3. Why is it good to hire a younger person for a job? Give your opinion.
4. Why is it good to hire an older person for a job? Give your opinion.
5. If you were in Ruben's position, what would you do? Would you stay in Mexico or come to America? Give your opinion. Mention more than one reason.

What's Your Story?

In your country, what types of jobs do people over 40 find?

Tom McKitterick, Impact Visuals

A Busy Time

On Fridays and Saturdays the work was very hard in my family's store in Puerto Rico. My father got up early, went to the store, and got everything ready for the day.

The people bought so much food! Some people made a list of what they wanted. We knew what to get for them. But some people didn't write a list. We had to ask them everything!

For example, the same three old men always came on those days.

"Do you want rice?" we asked. "Do you want a chicken, a hen?"

"Oh yes," they said. "Yes, yes."

"Do you want fish?"

"Yes, yes."

"Do you want tomato sauce, salt?"

"No."

It was hard to guess what the customers wanted. It was better when I got a list.

Some people stopped in and asked for beer or for something to mix with whiskey, like Coke or orange juice. When we had to sell them just one item, we lost time.

Sometimes people even got angry because they were in a hurry. "I want it fast!" they said. "I have to do this, I have to do that!"

"You have to wait!" I told them.

People paid with cash, with checks, or with welfare food coupons. People paid on credit, too. We had to stop what we were doing and write up their bill. Sometimes we didn't have time to eat!

—**Maria Velasquez**
Puerto Rico

Comprehension

True or False

Write **T** or **F** for true or false.

_____ 1. Maria's family always had a day off on Saturdays.

_____ 2. Fridays and Saturdays were busy times because people bought
so much food.

_____ 3. Maria's family liked people to bring lists of things to buy.

_____ 4. The store sold whiskey.

_____ 5. People had to pay by cash only.

_____ 6. The customers were always polite.

Language Skills

Vocabulary Review

1. Please write the names of five foods from the story.

_____

_____

_____

_____

_____

2. Write the names of four things to drink from the story.

    _____

    _____

    _____

    _____

3. Now write the names of four ways to pay from the story.

    _____

    _____

    _____

    _____

Structure Practice: Singular and Plural

Find spellings for plurals of the words below in the story. Some have an **-s** and some do not. Some have different spellings. Some do not change at all.

1. man   _____   6. salt   _____

2. check   _____   7. day   _____

3. rice   _____   8. person   _____

4. Saturday   _____   9. coupon _____

5. customer _____ 10. fish   _____

Structure Practice: Past Tense

Write the past tense forms for the verbs below.

When I was in Puerto Rico, we always _____ early on

(get up)

Fridays and Saturdays. Many people _____ in and

(come)

_____ food on those days. Some people _____

(buy)   (make)

a list, but some people didn't. We _____ a lot of time with

(lose)

these people. Some people _____ cash. Some people used

(pay)

checks. When people were in a hurry, they sometimes _____

(get)

angry. But we _____ them to wait.

(tell)

Punctuation

Study the punctuation marks below. Add the missing punctuation to these sentences.
Look at the story again if you need help.

?   .   " "   ,   !

Do you want rice we asked Do you want a chicken a hen

Oh yes they said Yes yes

Sometimes people even got angry because they were in a hurry I want it fast

they said I have to do this I have to do that

People paid with cash with checks and with welfare food coupons People paid

on credit too

Structure Practice

The form of an auxiliary verb or helping verb, changes when the tense changes.

Examples: Some people <u>didn't</u> write a list.

We <u>had to</u> remember everything.

You <u>have to</u> wait!

We <u>could</u> check what to get for them.

Note that when the helping verb is in the past, the main verb is still in the base form. Now finish these helping verb sentences with your own words.

1. Every month I have to pay _____.

2. When I was a child, I often had to visit _____.

3. When I was in school in my country, I could do _____ well.

4. Before I came to school today, I had to _____.

5. Last weekend I didn't _____.

6. After I study more English, I can _____.

Follow-up

A Closer Look

Choose the answer that you think completes the sentence best. The answers are not stated directly in the story, but you can figure them out.

1. On Fridays and Saturdays Maria probably
   a. was happy because she saw so many old friends.
   b. didn't like working so hard but liked making money for the family.
   c. got up late and went fishing.

2. Food lists helped Maria because
   a. she learned what people liked to eat.
   b. she could go find things quickly, not one at a time.
   c. old men don't ask good questions.

3. Sometimes Maria's family didn't have time to eat because

    a. they were too busy.

    b. they were too fat.

    c. they wanted to go someplace on their day off.

4. On Saturday night Maria's father probably

    a. was tired and went home to bed after the store closed.

    b. stayed in the store to get everything ready for Sunday.

    c. took his family to a restaurant for a long dinner.

Let's Talk about It

1. Why did Maria's father always get up early on Fridays and Saturdays?

2. Why was it better for customers to bring a list?

3. Why was it difficult when customers didn't bring a list?

4. What problem did the store have when people were on their way to other places?

5. What problem did the store have when people were in a hurry?

What's Your Story?

What's a busy time where you work? Tell about what happens during that time.

Evan Johnson, Impact Visuals

Learning on the Job

I work as a receptionist and office manager at Centro Pedro Claver, a community center in Philadelphia. I like to meet and help the people who come there. I love my job.

I learned my job by watching other people. Some things I taught myself. Asking questions and getting to know people helped. My supervisor also taught me about the job. For example, she showed me how to operate the copy machine. I helped her, too, by answering the telephone and starting a system for people to sign in and out when they came for programs. I learned how to take checks and make receipts. It was also helpful to learn spoken English. In my job I speak Spanish, but I need to know some English, too.

My first office job was at Project Ayuda, a program for senior citizens. I started there as a volunteer. After that,

I got paid for four hours a day, because I was always there on time and never took a sick day. I cleaned a little. I also answered the phone and took people's messages. People got to know me. That's how I got the job at Centro Pedro Claver. Because I was a good worker and the people at Centro Pedro Claver knew about me, I was offered a full-time job.

This year I will be in charge of a summer program for 80 children. I will give them their lunch and a snack, and I will also keep an attendance list. Because public assistance pays for the children to come, a caseworker will check the attendance list.

This story is not finished. I will continue to learn new things. Every day is an opportunity to learn.

—**Nelly Mariotta**
Puerto Rico

Comprehension

True or False

Write **T** or **F** for true or false.

_____ 1. Nelly learned all about her job from her supervisor.

_____ 2. Nelly's supervisor started a new system for signing people in and out.

_____ 3. Nelly has to speak only English at her job.

_____ 4. Centro Pedro Claver is a program for senior citizens.

_____ 5. Nelly got her job at Centro Pedro Claver because of her work at Project Ayuda.

_____ 6. There will be 800 children in the summer program.

_____ 7. Public assistance pays for the children in her summer program.

Time Sequence

Place the numbers **1** through **5** in front of each event from Nelly's story to show the order in which things happened.

_____ Nelly got paid for part-time work at Project Ayuda.

_____ Nelly got a full-time job at Centro Pedro Claver.

_____ Nelly's supervisor taught her how to use the copy machine.

_____ Nelly volunteered at Project Ayuda.

_____ Nelly was put in charge of a summer program for 80 children.

Locating Information

Nelly talks about the three things listed below without using those exact terms in her story. Look back at the story to find out where Nelly tells about her experience of each. Briefly write about what she says.

1. on-the-job training

   _____

2. duties and responsibilities at Project Ayuda

   _____

3. duties and responsibilities at Centro Pedro Claver

   _____

Language Skills

Word Families

Read and study each set of words:

operation	registration	attendance	assistance
operate(d)	register(ed)	attend(ed)	assist(ed)

Read the following sentences. Circle the correct form of the word in parentheses.

1. They run a very successful business (operate, operation).

2. I want to (register, registration) my child for summer camp.

3. Nelly learned how to (operate, operation) the copy machine.

4. If you need some (assist, assistance), I'll be glad to help you.

5. (Register, Registration) will take place on Saturday from 9 AM to 12 noon.

6. The teacher checked the names on the (attend, attendance) list.

7. Before you (attend, attendance) classes, you have to fill out a (register, registration) form.

Structure Practice: Past Tense

Write the past tense forms for the verbs below.

Alfredo _____ to the United States in 1986. He already
(come)

_____ English, so he _____ computer
(know)   (take)

classes at the community college in town. After a year, he _____
(get)

a job in data entry at a small electronics company. His supervisor

_____ him a lot about the new job. But Alfredo wanted to
(teach)

continue studying. While he was working, he also _____ some
(take)

more computer classes, and his company _____ his tuition.
(pay)

Alfredo _____ he was lucky to get this work benefit.
(know)

Structure Practice

Sometimes the word **by** in the middle of a sentence introduces a phrase that tells
how the first part of the sentence was done.

Examples: I learned my job **by** watching other people.
                 I helped her **by** answering the telephone.

Complete the sentences below using your own words.

1. I got my first job by _____

   _____.

2. I practice my English by _____

_____.

3. I help my coworkers by _____

_____.

4. I would like to help other people by _____

_____.

Follow-up

A Closer Look

Circle the answer which you think best explains the meaning of the underlined word in each sentence. Look back at the story if you need help.

1. I like to meet the people who come <u>there</u>.
   - a. Centro Pedro Claver
   - b. Project Ayuda
   - c. Philadelphia
   - d. Puerto Rico

2. I helped <u>her</u> by answering the telephone.
   - a. Nelly
   - b. Nelly's girlfriend
   - c. Nelly's supervisor
   - d. Nelly's mother

3. After <u>that</u>, I got paid for four hours.
   - a. working as a volunteer
   - b. working at Centro Pedro Claver
   - c. starting a sign-in system
   - d. learning to speak English

4. ...because I was always <u>there</u> on time.
   - a. Project Ayuda
   - b. Centro Pedro Claver
   - c. English class
   - d. summer camp

5. <u>That</u>'s how I got the job at Centro Pedro Claver.
   a. learning to speak English
   b. helping as a volunteer
   c. people getting to know her
   d. registering children for a summer program

Let's Talk about It
   1. How was Nelly active in learning her job?
   2. How did Nelly's volunteer work lead to a paid job?
   3. Why do you think Nelly loves her job?
   4. Why was Nelly given a job at Centro Pedro Claver?
   5. What does Nelly mean when she says, "Every day is an opportunity to learn"?

Thinking about the Story
   What can you learn from being a volunteer?

   How did Nelly take advantage of opportunities?

   Nelly says she was a "good worker." In your opinion, what are the characteristics of a good worker?

What's Your Story?
   How did you learn your job?

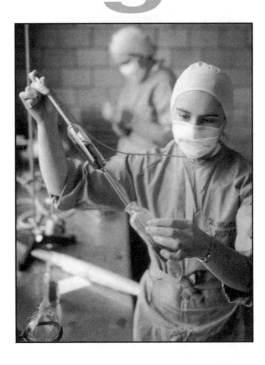

Getting Ahead

I came to the United States from Czechoslovakia many years ago. When I came to this country, my English was not so good. I did sewing, and also some piecework in the mills. It was hot, and I used to dream that the machines were running me over.

When my English got better, I joined the union. But then I left the factory and worked as a volunteer in a city hospital so that I could learn a new job. The doctor in the laboratory liked my work. He told me to go to City Hall and take a civil service test for work in histology. Histology is the study of body tissue. I passed the test and became a paid trainee in the histology lab. Six months later, I took another test at City Hall and became a histology technician.

Nowadays you need to study in college to do this kind of work. But I was able to learn a lot on the job. Because I worked in a city hospital, I could take tests at City Hall. That was a long time ago. In 1971 I was able to take some university courses, and then I became a registered histology technician. Before I retired, I worked at the County Medical Examiner's Office. I loved my work.

—**Martha Manjulowicz**
Czechoslovakia

Comprehension

True or False

Write **T** or **F** for true or false.

_____ 1. Martha came to the United States from Australia.

_____ 2. Martha enjoyed her factory job.

_____ 3. Martha worked as a volunteer to learn a new job.

_____ 4. Martha did not pass the tests at City Hall.

_____ 5. Martha had to take special classes in order to work in the histology lab.

_____ 6. Nowadays you have to study in college to become a histology technician.

Complete the Sentence

Fill in the blanks with the appropriate words and phrases from the story.

When I came to this country, I did sewing and _____ in the

mills. I used to dream that the _____ were running me over.

When my English got better, I joined the _____. Then I worked

as a _____ in a city hospital. There, a doctor told me to take a

_____ _____ _____

for work in histology. I became a paid _____ in the histology

lab. Later, I took another test at _____

_____ and became a histology _____.

Language Skills

Structure Practice: Past Tense

Write the past tense forms for the verbs below.

When I _____ here, I _____ a job
                                 (come)   (get)

working in a factory. But I wanted to be an engineer. So after a year, I

_____ the factory and entered a training program. When I
          (leave)

finished that program, I _____ a technician with an electronics
                               (become)

company.

While I was working, I _____ to school. I _____
                               (go)   (take)

engineering courses at the college in my town. It _____ hard
                                                   (be)

to work and study at the same time, but my children _____
                                                        (tell)

me, "Mom, we know you can do it!" They _____ very proud of
                                                  (be)

me when I finally graduated with my degree in engineering.

Vocabulary: Opposite Meanings

Read the following word pairs. Study the opposite meanings.

    volunteer—paid

    loved—hated

    passed—failed

Complete the sentences below with words from the word pairs above. The first one is done for you.

1. Martha worked as a volunteer. She did not get _____paid_____.

2. Martha loved her lab work. She _____ her sewing job.

3. Martha passed her tests. If she had _____, she could not have gotten a paid job.

4. A paid job is different from being a _____.

5. Martha hated her sewing job, but _____ her work in the lab.

6. After the student failed the first test, he studied hard and _____ the second test.

Structure Practice: Compound Sentences

Notice how the word **and** is used to join words and phrases in this example.

    Example: a. I did sewing.

                   b. I did piecework in the mills.

              I did sewing and piecework in the mills.

Combine each set of short sentences below to make one long sentence.

1. a. I left the factory.
   b. I worked as a volunteer in a city hospital.

    _____

_____

2. a. The doctor told me to go to City Hall.
   b. The doctor told me to take the civil service test.

   _____

3. a. I passed the test.
   b. I became a paid trainee in the lab.

   _____

4. a. Six months later, I took another test.
   b. I became a histology technician.

   _____

Follow-up

Let's Talk about It
1. How do you think Martha felt about her first job?
2. Why did she work as a volunteer?
3. Who encouraged Martha to take a test to become a histology technician?
4. How did Martha advance in her career?
5. How did she learn her job?
6. How do people today get jobs like Martha's?

Thinking about the Story
Was it easier to get a job when Martha first came to the United States?
Why or why not?

What's Your Story?
How do people get ahead in your line of work? Is any special training or testing required?

THE BETTMANN ARCHIVE

Working

During World War II, I worked in a munitions factory in occupied France. Women from France, Belgium, Russia, and other countries worked there.

We all had to drink milk. It coated our throats and protected us from the dynamite powder fumes. Those were hard times, the war years, but we were young and didn't know anything else. Even though we were always being watched, at night we would sneak out and have parties.

After the war, I came to America. I got a job at the Bulova watch factory with my brother. I also made new friends, and they helped me when I tried to learn English. In those days, it was pretty easy to get a job whether you knew English or not. There were more factories and more jobs.

After working in the watch factory for a few years, I worked in a paper box factory and on the packaging line for the Elizabeth Arden company. Still, it's hard to live in a country when you don't know the language.

Later on, I worked for the French Line, the company that owned France's passenger ship. The ship was called the Liberty. She was very grand and very beautiful.

At my job, I did bookkeeping and typing. This was a step up for me, and I got free trips on the Liberty. Knowing French and English helped me do that job.

Today I am retired and living in France. I'm glad I lived in America. But I am glad, now, to be back home.

—**Georgette Lucce**
France

Comprehension

True or False

Write **T** or **F** for true or false.

_____ 1. Even during the war, Georgette and the other women at the munitions factory had fun.

_____ 2. In the United States, Georgette couldn't get a job until she learned English.

_____ 3. Georgette found life in the United States hard at first because she didn't know English.

_____ 4. Knowing two languages helped Georgette do her job with the French Line.

_____ 5. Georgette paid a lot of money to travel on the French Line's ship, the Liberty.

Time Sequence

Place the numbers **1** through **7** in front of each event in Georgette's story to show the order in which things happened.

_____ Georgette worked for Elizabeth Arden.

_____ Georgette learned office work.

_____ During World War II, Georgette worked in a munitions factory.

_____ Later on, Georgette worked for the French Line.

_____ Georgette got a job at a watch factory.

_____ Georgette moved back to France.

_____ After the war, Georgette came to the United States.

Language Skills

Structure Practice: Time Signals
Complete the following sentences with your own words.

1. I grew up during _____.

2. In those days _____.

3. When I first came to America _____.

4. Later on _____.

5. Now _____.

Same Word—Different Meanings
Some words in English have more than one meaning. Read each sentence and write the meaning of the underlined word in the blank that follows.

1. Even though we were always being <u>watched</u>, at night we would sneak out.

   _____

2. I got a job at the Bulova <u>watch</u> factory.

   _____

3. I worked on the packaging <u>line</u> for Elizabeth Arden.

   _____

4. Later on, I got a job working for the French <u>Line</u>.

   _____

Follow-up

A Closer Look

Circle the answer which you think best explains the meaning of the underlined word in each sentence. Look back at the story if you need help.

1. Those were hard times.
   a. winters in France
   b. Georgette's years at school
   c. the years during World War II
   d. the years after World War II

2. ...but we were young and didn't know anything else.
   a. Georgette and her brother
   b. Georgette and the other women at the munitions factory
   c. Georgette and her friends in America
   d. Georgette and the other women at Elizabeth Arden

3. In those days, it was pretty easy to get a job.
   a. during the summer
   b. during World War II
   c. during the years before the war
   d. during the years after World War II

4. This job was a step up for me.
   a. Georgette's job at the munitions factory
   b. Georgette's job at the watch factory
   c. Georgette's job at Elizabeth Arden
   d. Georgette's job at the French Line

5. She was very grand and very beautiful.
   a. Georgette's mother
   b. the Statue of Liberty
   c. the ship, the Liberty
   d. Georgette's English teacher

Let's Talk about It

1. How did Georgette manage to have fun during World War II?
2. Why was it easy to get a job in the United States after World War II, even without knowing English?
3. Was it easy or difficult for Georgette to adjust to life in the United States? Give reasons for your answers.
4. Why was the job at the French Line a "step up" for Georgette?
5. Did she enjoy her work at the French Line? Why?
6. Why do you think Georgette is glad to be back in France?

Thinking about the Story

Georgette says "it's hard to live in a country when you don't know the language." In your opinion, what makes it hard to live in a place when you don't know the language?

What's Your Story?

Do you know someone who has held many different jobs? Write about that person. If this is true for you, you can tell your own story.

11

Patty DiRienzo

My Work Dream

I want to learn English and get a better job. I would also like to study painting—nature, landscapes. I'd love to work just on my own, not for a company.

Whenever I have free time at home, I love to paint. And I'm proud to say that people like my pictures. I have already sold several of my paintings in America. Most of my paintings show American subjects, and especially the beautiful American landscapes. I don't paint Mexican subjects very much at all right now. I don't know why.

In the future I'll dedicate myself to painting, maybe all day. I don't want to work in a factory making dresses all my life. I won't wait to retire before I start to paint.

I didn't paint in Mexico. It's a new thing for me. But it's not just a hobby. It's something that I feel inside me. A while ago, I started to feel the necessity to make something. I need to do it.

I want to spend all my time painting. But I don't know when I'll be able to do this, because I need to learn English well first. After my language skills are strong, I will get serious about studying painting!

—**Ruben Amaro**
Mexico

Comprehension

True or False

Write **T** or **F** for true or false.

_____ 1. Ruben's work dream is to work for a large company.

_____ 2. The problem with Ruben's work dream is that no one likes his paintings.

_____ 3. Ruben might be upset if you called his painting dream a hobby.

_____ 4. A visitor to Ruben's home might see many paintings of beautiful Mexican landscapes.

_____ 5. Ruben wants to study more English because he wants to get a better job.

_____ 6. Ruben painted for many years before he came to the United States.

Multiple Choice

Circle the best way to complete each sentence.

1. Ruben likes to paint
   a. houses.   c. portraits.
   b. landscapes.   d. cars.

2. Ruben is proud because
   a. his father was a painter.   c. he loves to paint.
   b. he was a painter in Mexico.   d. people like his pictures.

3. Ruben has been painting
   a. only since he came to America. c. since he lost his job.
   b. all his life.   d. for many years.

4. Ruben wants to improve his English because
   a. he might want to read books in English about painting.
   b. he needs to get a good job and earn money so he can paint.
   c. in this way he will become a better dressmaker.
   d. he won't have anything else to do when he retires.

Language Skills

Word Families

Write adjective forms for these nouns. All the words are in Ruben's story.

1. pride _____   4. freedom_____

2. beauty _____   5. strength_____

3. seriousness_____ 6. Mexico _____

Structure Practice: Prepositions

Write the words below into the story. You may use a word more than once.

for   of   about   in   at

    Ruben would like to study landscape painting. He paints whenever he has free

time _____ home. He has already sold some

_____ his paintings. Most _____ his work

shows American landscapes. _____ Mexico, he never painted.

It's a new skill _____ him. But he doesn't want to spend the

rest of his life working _____ a factory. He doesn't like working

_____ a company. When his English is better, he can be more

serious _____ studying for his work dream.

Vocabulary Review

Write the words below into the story.

dedicate   hobby   nature   landscapes   serious

My _____ is taking long walks through the countryside.

I enjoy seeing the beautiful, unspoiled _____ near my home. Some

people don't think it is important to protect _____. But the

problems facing the natural world are very _____. When I

retire, I want to _____ the rest of my life to solving these

problems.

Structure Practice: Auxiliary Verbs

Write the full form of the underlined auxiliary verbs, or helping verbs, and main verbs in the sentences below. The first one is done for you.

1. I'd love to work on my own.

   _would love_____

2. I don't paint Mexican subjects.

   _____

3. In the future I'll dedicate myself to painting.

   _____

4. I won't wait to retire before I start to paint.

   _____

5. I didn't paint in Mexico.

   _____

6. I <u>don't want</u> to work in a factory all my life.

_____

7. I don't know when I'<u>ll be</u> able to do this.

_____

Follow-up

Let's Talk about It

1. Why does Ruben continue to paint? Give two reasons.
2. What does Ruben plan to do to achieve his work dream? What do you think he should do?
3. Why did Ruben start to paint after coming to America? Why does he paint more American subjects than Mexican subjects now? Give your opinion.
4. Why is Ruben unhappy working in a factory? Give your opinion.
5. Is it better to work for a company or to work alone, as Ruben wants to do? Give your opinion.

What's Your Story?

What plans or dreams do you have for your future? What can you do to make those plans or dreams come true?

12

Kirk Condyles, Impact Visuals

A Better Life

I came to the United States to work. I wanted to send money home so my family could buy land. I'm waiting for a green card, but it is taking a long time.

My family is very poor. I remember my sisters each had only one simple cloth to wrap around themselves. They washed their cloths out at night in boiling water, because sometimes we had no money to buy soap. Sometimes we had no oil to cook with, so we had to boil the food.

When I came to New York, all I had was a phone number of a family I could work for. I was so excited. I just wanted to come to America.

I worked for the family for two years. They didn't pay me, but they bought me clothes. I was so happy because I had food to eat and soap to wash my clothes.

Later, I worked for another family. I took care of their children. I lived in their house, but they didn't like me to be around on my day off. I had no place to go on my day off. I got very sick in the winter because I was not used to the cold.

Now I work as a companion to an old lady. I have friends, too. But I still get sick in the winter. I can't send any money home because I have to pay my own medical bills. It's been really hard for me in America, but it's worse at home.

I am learning to read and write English. I know how to speak English, Swahili, and Madgari, but I never learned to read and write any language. I'm very glad to be learning. At home, I would never have this opportunity.

—Rose E.
Kenya

Comprehension

True or False

Write **T** or **F** for true or false.

_____ 1. Rose came to the United States to get married.

_____ 2. Rose's family is very poor.

_____ 3. Rose didn't want to come to America.

_____ 4. Rose already knew people in New York when she arrived.

_____ 5. The weather in New York made Rose ill.

_____ 6. Rose can speak three languages.

_____ 7. Rose works in an office now.

Time Sequence

Place the numbers **1** through **5** in front of each event from Rose's story to show the order in which things happened.

_____ Rose got a job working as companion to an old lady.

_____ Rose came to the United States.

_____ Rose and her family had no oil to cook with.

_____ Rose worked for a family for two years, receiving only food and clothes.

_____ Rose took care of a family's children and got sick from the winter cold.

Language Skills

Structure Practice: Simple Present and Present Continuous Tense
Circle the correct verb form.

1. I (have, am having) friends in America.

2. I (learn, am learning) to read and write English.

3. I still (get, am getting) sick in the winter.

4. I (have, am having) to pay my doctor bills.

5. I (wait, am waiting) for a green card.

6. It (takes, is taking) a long time to get my green card.

Structure Practice
The word **because** is usually followed by a reason. Read the following sentences from the story.

They washed their clothes out at night in boiling water, because sometimes the family didn't have money to buy soap.

I was happy because I had food to eat and soap to wash my clothes.

I can't send money home because I have to pay my own medical bills.

Now finish the sentences below with your own reasons.

1. I (like, don't like) living here because _____

_____.

2. I miss my native country because _____

_____.

3. I have to go shopping because _____

_____.

4. _____

because the weather here is too _____.

5. _____

because I'm learning English.

Follow-up

Let's Talk about It

1. Why did Rose come to the United States?
2. How did her first employer treat her?
3. How did she feel about that job?
4. What is good about Rose's life in the United States?
5. What is not good about Rose's life in the United States?

Thinking about the Story

With all the difficulties Rose has in America, do you think she made the right choice in coming here? Give reasons for your answer.

What's Your Story?

What were some good things that happened for you when you first came to the United States? What were some things that gave you problems when you first came to this country?

Have you ever been unhappy in a job?

Patty DiRienzo

Disappointment

Sometimes people in America don't like foreigners. My husband had a bad experience. Many years ago he took a job developing photographs, even though it was below his education level. His work was always very good and very clear. But one day, he was accused of doing bad work. Someone had switched his prints with a bad batch of photographs. The manager and other staff members forced him to take the blame. He said, "Martha, they don't like me." He was very depressed. He left that job and became a guard at a bank. But he wasn't treated well there, either.

This is what sometimes happens to people when they come here. They get so hurt and disgusted that they just stay home and collect their unemployment check or stay on welfare. But staying home doesn't help, either. The children do not learn the importance of work. They do not learn perseverance.

People sometimes admire me because I studied hard, learned English, worked hard, and got a good job. But, as for me, I felt like I had no choice. I just did what I had to do.

—**Martha Manjulowicz**
Czechoslovakia

Comprehension

True or False

Write **T** or **F** for true or false.

_____ 1. Martha's husband knew how to develop photographs.

_____ 2. One day, Martha was accused of doing bad work.

_____ 3. Martha's husband became very depressed.

_____ 4. Martha's husband was treated well in his job as a bank guard.

_____ 5. Martha stays home and collects unemployment.

_____ 6. Martha has perseverance.

Complete the Sentence

Fill in the blanks with the appropriate words and phrases from the story.

Sometimes people in America don't like _____. My

husband had a bad _____. He took a job

_____ photographs, even though it was below his

_____ _____. His work was

always very _____ and very _____.

But one day, he was _____ of doing bad work. Someone

had _____ his prints with a _____

_____ of photographs.

Language Skills

Vocabulary

Circle the correct word.

1. Martha's husband was (accused, depressed) of doing bad work.

2. Martha's husband took the (blame, perseverance) for someone else's mistake.

3. When people get (disgusted, switched), they sometimes lose hope.

4. It takes (blame, perseverance) to get ahead.

5. Martha's husband (accused, switched) jobs at least once.

6. Some people (admired, disgusted) Martha for working hard.

Word Families

Write the noun form for these verbs. The first one is in the story.

1. educate   _____

2. accuse   _____

3. admire   _____

4. immigrate   _____

5. operate   _____

6. inspire   _____

7. imagine   _____

8. inflate   _____

Structure Practice: Compound Verbs

Combine each set of short sentences below to make one long sentence. Use **and** to combine the appropriate words and phrases.

1. a. They just stay home.
   b. They collect an unemployment check.

   _____

2. a. She came to America.
   b. She looked for an apartment.

   _____

3. a. He worked during the day.
   b. He went to school at night.

   _____

4. a. I studied hard.   c. I worked hard.
   b. I learned English.   d. I got a good job.

   _____

Follow-up

A Closer Look

Read the sentences below. Circle the word or phrase that means the same as the underlined word. Refer to the story if you need help.

1. It was below his education level.

   a. coming to America   c. getting welfare
   b. developing photographs   d. switching jobs

2. "Martha, they don't like me."

   a. Americans
   b. the people at the bank
   c. the manager and staff at the photography studio
   d. Martha's family

3. He was not treated well <u>there</u>, either.
   a. at the photography studio
   b. at the bank
   c. in the hospital
   d. in America

4. <u>This</u> is what sometimes happens when people come here.
   a. they find good jobs
   b. their life is better
   c. they forget their families
   d. they get hurt and disgusted

Let's Talk about It

1. Why do people admire Martha?
2. How does Martha feel about what she did?
3. Why did Martha's husband leave his job with the photography company?
4. According to Martha, why do some foreigners become depressed in the United States?
5. Is Martha's husband working now? Why or why not? Give reasons for your answers.
6. Why does she say unemployment is not good for children? Do you agree?
7. In your opinion why does Martha say she had no choice?

Thinking about the Story

Martha says that if parents don't work, their children don't learn perseverance. What are some ways that parents can teach perseverance to their children?

What's Your Story?

Tell a story about your own or someone else's perseverance.

14

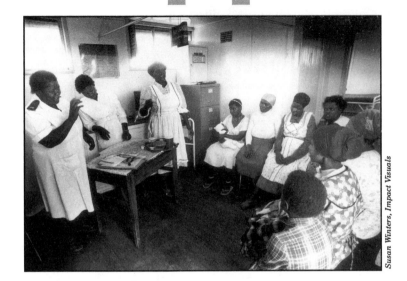

Susan Winters, Impact Visuals

Helping People

Before I came here to the United States, I was in the Sudan. During this period of time I worked as an advanced health worker in a refugee camp clinic owned by the United Nations.

This camp is in the eastern part of the Sudan, almost at the border of Ethiopia. Thousands and thousands of Ethiopians have escaped from their homeland due to war and hunger. Now they live in refugee camps.

There are many refugee camps in the eastern Sudan. The refugees get supplies from the United Nations, but the donations can't cover all of their expenses, so the refugees work on farms and do other cheap labor to survive. The United Nations also provides medical assistance for the refugees.

This area is a tropical zone, and so there are special types of disease. My work was to give I.M. or I.V. injections, dress wounds, do suturing, etc. I also distributed tablets for the doctors' prescriptions.

I was very interested in this work because it gives assistance to the people. I was especially happy when the patient was cured of his disease. The health worker is respected by both the community and the patient.

After working in this clinic for three years, I now have quite satisfactory experience in the field. If I succeed in my GED examination, I plan to go to college and study in this medical field.

—**Abreham Hadera**
Ethiopia

Comprehension

True or False

Write **T** or **F** for true or false.

_____ 1. There are many refugee camps in the Sudan because that country has much war and hunger.

_____ 2. Special kinds of disease develop in tropical zones like the Sudan.

_____ 3. Abreham wants to study engineering in college.

_____ 4. The United Nations pays all expenses for the refugees in the Sudan.

_____ 5. There are farms in the eastern part of the Sudan.

_____ 6. The camp where Abreham worked was owned by the government of the Sudan.

Multiple Choice

1. From past to present, the countries in which Abreham has lived have been
   a. the Sudan, Angola, America.
   b. Ethiopia, the Sudan, America.
   c. the Sudan, Ethiopia, America.
   d. Ethiopia, Angola, the Sudan, America.

2. A health worker does not
   a. give injections.
   b. distribute tablets.
   c. suture wounds.
   d. write prescriptions.

3. The Sudan is
   a. a tropical country near Ethiopia.
   b. between Ethiopia and the United States of America.
   c. a good place to take the GED exam.
   d. a country with too many diseases.

4. The United Nations helps refugees by
   a. finding them jobs on farms near refugee camps.
   b. donating basic supplies and providing health care.
   c. training them to be advanced health care workers.
   d. giving them all the money they need to find new homes.

Language Skills

Vocabulary Review

Study the underlined words in the sentences below. Finish the sentences with your own words.

1. One country with <u>tropical</u> weather in Asia or South America is

   _____.

2. One time I had to get a <u>prescription</u> medicine because I was sick with

   _____.

3. A part of the body where people often get <u>injections</u> is

   _____.

4. One good thing to <u>donate</u> when people need help is _____.

5. People go to a <u>clinic</u> when they are _____.

Word Families

Write the noun forms for these verbs. The first four are in the story.

1. examine _____   5. describe _____

2. inject _____   6. determine_____

3. prescribe _____   7. protect _____

4. donate _____   8. infect _____

Structure Practice

Write the connecting words below into the story. Look back at Abreham's story if you need help.

   because   If   During   also   before   After

Abreham lived in the Sudan _____ he came to America.

_____ this time, he worked in a refugee camp clinic. He gave

injections and dressed wounds. He _____ did suturing. He

liked this work a lot _____ he was giving help to people.

_____ three years, he came to America. He has much

experience now. _____ he can get his GED, he will continue to

study health work.

Follow-up

A Closer Look

Circle the answer which you think best explains the meaning of the underlined word(s) in each sentence. Look back at the story if you need help.

1. During this period of time I worked as an advanced health worker...
   - a. my childhood
   - b. my years in the Sudan
   - c. my years in the United States
   - d. my years at the United Nations

2. This camp is in the eastern part of the Sudan...
   - a. the refugee camp
   - b. Abreham's new home
   - c. Ethiopia
   - d. the United States

3. Now they live in refugee camps.
   - a. people from the Sudan
   - b. people from Ethiopia
   - c. Abreham's family
   - d. United Nations workers

4. ...the donations can't cover all of <u>their</u> expenses.
   a. the United Nations
   b. Abreham's family
   c. the refugees
   d. the doctors at the clinic

5. I was very interested in <u>this work</u>...
   a. health work
   b. refugee camp work
   c. United Nations work
   d. teaching

Let's Talk about It

1. What were some of Abreham's job responsibilities as a health worker in the Sudan? Give at least two examples.
2. Why did Abreham like his work? Give at least two reasons.
3. What experiences from his past will help Abreham when he tries to continue his medical career in America? Please give your opinion.
4. What problems will Abreham face when he tries to continue his medical career in America? Give your opinion.

What's Your Story?

What experiences from your past helped prepare you for your job? What other training did you get, or will you need to get in the future?

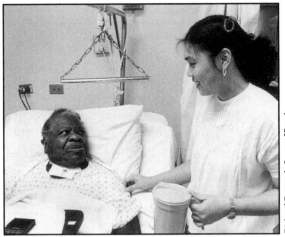

Richard Bermack, Impact Visuals

Being Accepted

I earned my bachelor's degree in nursing in Puerto Rico. In college I was very popular and well liked. I felt like I had a bright future waiting for me.

I came to Miami because I needed a change. I had not yet taken my nursing boards, so I got a job as a nurse's assistant in a home for the elderly. It was a lot of hard work.

Later, I got a job as a graduate nurse in a small hospital. There, the supervisors made me go through two orientation periods, and I still didn't get all of the training that was given to another graduate nurse, who was white. This was my first experience of prejudice.

A few months later, I moved to New York. I passed my nursing boards, and got a job at Mt. Sinai Hospital. There I found myself working very hard in a very large hospital with many different kinds of people—white, black, Indian, Asian, and others. I was not popular there. There was only one other Hispanic nurse.

What impressed me was that when I treated staff and patients with love, the differences among us of race, color, or background no longer got in the way.

I had a terminally ill patient who was a Hasidic Jew. We had a wonderful relationship. His wife brought some beautiful sweaters as gifts for some of the nurses. She gave me first choice, so I received a beautiful pink sweater. I know it was the love and the respect between us that made the difference.

—Coral Andino
Puerto Rico

Comprehension

True or False

Write **T** or **F** for true or false.

_____ 1. Coral came to America because her father needed her.

_____ 2. As a graduate nurse Coral got the same training as all the other nurses at the hospital.

_____ 3. Coral was very popular at Mt. Sinai Hospital.

_____ 4. Coral found that love helped improve relations with both staff members and patients.

_____ 5. Coral gave a sweater to the wife of her Hasidic patient.

Time Sequence

Number the events in Coral's story from **1** to **7** to show the order in which they happened.

_____ Coral got a job at Mt. Sinai Hospital.

_____ Coral got a job in a small hospital.

_____ Coral worked as a nurse's assistant in a home for the elderly.

_____ Coral passed her nursing boards.

_____ Coral had to go through two orientation periods.

_____ Coral got a bachelor's degree in nursing.

_____ Coral moved to New York.

Complete the Sentence

Fill in the blanks with the appropriate words and phrases from the story.

I earned my _____ _____ in nursing in

Puerto Rico. In college I was very _____ and well liked. I felt

like I had a _____ _____ waiting for me.

I came to Miami because I needed a _____. I had not yet

taken my _____ _____, so I got a job as a

_____ _____ in a home for the elderly.

Later, I got a job as a _____ _____ in a

small hospital. The supervisors made me go through two _____

periods, and I still didn't get all of the _____ that was given to

another _____ nurse, who was white. This was my first

experience of _____.

After I _____ my nursing boards, I got a job in Mt. Sinai

Hospital. What _____ me was that when I treated staff and

patients with love, the differences among us of _____,

_____, or _____ no longer got in the way.

Language Skills

Word Families

Read and study each set of words:

orientation	performance	supervisor	supervision
orient	perform	supervise	

Now circle the correct form of the word in parentheses in each sentence.

1. She will (perform, performance) to the best of her ability.

2. She worked under the (supervise, supervision) of the head nurse.

3. The director will (orient, orientation) the new employees.

4. Her (perform, performance) will be rated by the other doctors and nurses.

5. They (supervise, supervisor) a full staff.

6. The (orient, orientation) program for nurses was held in the hospital.

7. The (supervisor, supervision) gave very good directions.

Vocabulary Review

Coral mentions three places where she worked as a nurse. List them below.

_____

_____

_____

Can you name three other places where a nurse can get a job?

_____

_____

_____

Follow-up

Let's Talk about It

1. Why did Coral leave Puerto Rico?
2. What are the three different jobs Coral had when she first came to America? Explain what each job was like for her.
3. How do you think she felt about the staff and patients at Mt. Sinai Hospital?
4. What did Coral notice when she treated people with love and respect?

Thinking about the Story

In the story, Coral talks about prejudice. Describe Coral's experience of prejudice. Explain what prejudice means based on her experience.

Coral lists three differences among people that sometimes lead to prejudice. What are they? Can you think of any other reasons for prejudice?

What's Your Story?

What training did you get to prepare you for your job? Consider school preparation, training at work, and experience in your job.